THE ULTIMATE BUSINESS PLANNING GUIDE

THE ONLY GUIDE YOU WILL NEED TO WRITE
WINNING BUSIINESS PLANS FROM SCRATCH EVEN
IF ALL YOU HAVE IS A BUSINESS IDEA.

Business Planning Workbook & Business Plan
Templates Included

Ebenny Inc.

The Ultimate Business Planning Guide.

ISBN: 9781797064178

This eBook version was published by:
Ebenny Innovative Consults (Ebenny Inc.)
P.O.Box 125, Sango Ota
Ogun State, Nigeria.
ebennyinc@yahoo.com

CONTENTS

CHAPTER ONE

—ℬℭ—

BUSINESS PLANS:
THE WHAT & THE WHY

What is a Business Plan
A business plan is the working document that that is used to show all the important information for a business and clearly sets out the plan and strategies that will be used to run the company and ensure the business is profitable and achieves its objectives.

Getting a profitable business idea you want to run with can be sometimes daunting. And if eventually you get the idea, there are a million and one questions in your head. Can I pull this off? Will it work? What if it goes wrong? What if people do not buy my product or service?

Although, you can have a great idea, it does not mean that people will like it, want it, be willing to pay for it, or can afford it. You will also begin to consider the number of people who has that problem you are trying to solve. Is it just people on your street or the entire country?

That said, how much will it cost you to set up the business? So where do you get the money to start up? Would the business even be profitable? These and many more are the many tough questions that needs to be answered and a business plan helps you do just that.

SEVEN other reasons why you need to write a business plan

1. A business plan thinks about profitability from the very start and helps you drive the business forward so that it yields profits as planned.

2. A business plan helps you identify all the important aspects of a business and shows exactly how to handle every critical factor to ensure business success.

3. A business plan is vital for business that wants to stand the test of time and outlive their founders.

4. A business plan serves as the guide and benchmark for the business take off and growth

5. A business plan is a living document and helps you manage change as the company grows. It is not a permanent document that you can't change.

6. A business plan helps you communicate your company business goals and strategy and ensures your partners, staff and investors understand exactly your plans for the company.

7. A business plan is used to access funding, be it equity investments, loans or grants. It helps the intending investor understand what your business is about and evaluate the profitability.

With a business plan, it does not mean the business will 100% go according to plan. However, you can always use the plan to measure your progress and see if you are going in the direction you want. A business plan can be changed over time to reflect the new realities and trends in line with the company's objectives as set by the management.

A business plan can be simple and brief with as little as 3 pages and it can be complex running into tens of pages. Whatever the length is, a well-articulated business plan must answer the important questions.

CHAPTER TWO
—— 🙰🙵 ——

THE BUSINESS PLANNING PROCESS

The business planning process is the method of thinking through your business idea which helps to produce a business plan. To come up with a good business plan, you will need to think through the entire business planning process. Having said that, remember that the business plan is only a means to an end. It will be wrong to focus on the final output, which is the business plan itself. It is only a means to an end (business success) and not the end in itself.

This business planning process is very vital for business success. The business plan process helps you to take a panoramic view at the business and not just a microscopic view that most entrepreneurs have when developing a business idea. With business planning, you think of the future of the business and not just day to day operations. The planning process also helps you determine exactly what your business goals are and how you will define success. The business planning process helps you do all these from the very beginning, before you even start the business. It also helps you anticipate anything that could possible go wrong while and prepare well ahead of what you will do to manage them.

To put it all in perspective, to succeed in a business, you will need to think through the entire business planning process which you then document in a business plan. Thinking through the business planning process positions you for success and helps you easily write your business plans from scratch.

To take you through my unique Ebenny Inc Business Planning Process, I will ask some very important questions that you will need to provide thoughtful answers to. The goal here will be to think through and document your answers, thoughts and findings.

This planning guide has been written to help anyone, whether business savvy or not, develop the critical thinking patterns that help develop a successful business strategy.

To get results from going through the business planning process, you will need to do the following:

1. **Create Time**
    Set aside at least 10 minutes to do nothing else but think about each question. You can come up with better answers when you dedicate time and concentrate on just that one thing. More so, some of the questions will need you to reflect deeply and you will need to focus to do this.

2. **Get a Notepad**
    Make some note as you begin to think of your answers. While you should try to think hard to come up with relevant answers, it is important you do not really screen your responses here. Just put down every thought to paper. At some point, you will notice that you have answered related questions earlier, at those points, see

how your responses to the new question relate to your responses to the previous questions. You should also note down any striking patterns or correlation. Sometimes, I do this by drawing linking lines.

3. **Do active research**

   This is very important. It is the only way to get insight about information you are not previously aware of. With business planning comes the need to be factual and have actual figures, numbers and information, you cannot make guesses so you will sometimes have to dig for specific information that you need. Use Google which is likely on your fingertips. Ask other people who you think might have the answers. Now is a good time to put Facebook messenger and Whatsapp to use engaging in conversations that are beneficial. Join groups on Facebook and LinkedIn where you can get valuable insight and advice from people in your industry.

4. **Learn Passively**

   As you go about you day, ensure you catch yourself thinking about the question and your answers. Be aware of your environment and see if there would be anything that will throw some insight in to the question and answers that you have been thinking about.

5. **Do more Thinking**

   Just before you go to bed or go to sleep, you can maximize that brief moment to think a little bit more about your idea and business. Take that time to think about the insight and answers you are beginning to put together. You might have had a busy day and not given enough time to think hard about your business in responding to the business planning questions, This is the time to make up for it.

I think it is also a good thing that the next thing on your mind, after God is your business ideas. And if on some days, you cannot get some sleep because you can't stop thing about your idea. It is a good thing and a recipe for success.

The Business Planning Guide consists of 40 questions that you need to answer. If you can answer these questions to a certain level of detail, all you will need to do is to copy and paste your responses into a business plan template and you would have a complete business plan in minutes.

Answer to Details

Answer all 40 questions with as much detail as you can. For sake of clarification, let me make an illustration.

Question: What service do you offer?

Answer 1: I offer a laundry service

Answer 2: I offer a laundry service for busy professionals providing them with home/office pick-up and delivery options.

Answer 3: I offer a laundry service covering corporate wears, traditional attires and wedding dresses with an efficient process designed to meet the needs of busy professionals providing convenience and quality service through personalized care, home and office pick-up and delivery and various plans that are budget friendly.

Length of Time

This is up to you, you can decide to answer one question each day or you just take as many questions as you can answer in one day.

It is not about breezing through the questions but about thinking up quality answers for each of the questions. To answer some of the questions, you will need to brainstorm and do some deep thinking. To answer other questions, you will need to do an online search, speak with prospective customers or people already in the business or industry you want to go into. Some will require you carry out some level of market research while others will require an in-depth research into the business and industry.

Business Plan Process vs. Business Plan Template

When you begin to answer the 40 questions, it might not make sense at the beginning but trust me, it will all come together. At the end of the series, all you will need to do is to copy and paste your responses into a business plan template and you would have a complete business plan in minutes. The business planning process is the real deal and not the business plan template.

Making Assumptions: Conservative Estimates vs non-Conservative Estimates.

During the business planning process, aside some facts and figures that you will need to you will need to pull out from statistics and government or industry websites, you will also need to make a lot of assumptions simply because you have not done some things before so there is no way you will have the correct answer at hand. However, if you have done your market research well, you should be making an assumption that will be mostly accurate with the true picture of things when you begin.

When making assumptions, there is what is known as

Conservative Estimate: This assumption works with a worst case scenario. It envisages that things will pick up slowly and would not move rapidly.

Non-conservative Estimate: These estimates assumes a best case scenario when all is going extremely well

When answering the guide, you will need to be aware of both. If you make too conservative estimates, you might end up with a business plan that is not profitable and cannot generate enough funds.

If on the other hand, you are too optimistic, you can end up with a plan that is profitable on paper with expectations of having enough cash at hand to fund business transactions and this can create serious problems. If business does not go as planned, profits might dwindle leaving the firm without liquid cash to operate. It is valuable to mostly make assumptions somewhere between the conservative and non conservative estimates.

CHAPTER THREE

THE 40 QUESTION BUSINESS PLAN GUIDE™

They have been segmented into six various segments lettered A-F

A. BUSINESS/ VALUE PROPOSITION

1. What problem(s) are you solving for people?

People have problems right. People will always have needs and wants. Many times, the problems we face stand between us. You probably do yourself and truly man's needs are insatiable. What are the pain points that you are trying to solve?

2. What problem are solving for the world?

Sometimes the problem you are solving is a global problem and is not just limited to a population or group. You might be helping to fight malnutrition or prevent climate change. So is your idea solving a global problem?

3. Write out the unique solution you are proposing to solve the problems?

What is the exact solution you have to solve the problem you have identified? You should note that the more unique your solution is, the better it sounds as a viable business idea. This is because if everyone is offering that solution in the market, you will less likely stand out from the crowd except you can communicate the uniqueness in your own solution. It does not have to be a big uniqueness, sometimes a simple one as 'faster', or 'cheaper' might make the difference.

4. How is the solution different from other solutions in the market?

There might be different solutions to the problems you have identified and your competitors might already be providing a particular solution which you think you can improve on or provide better alternatives for?

5. What exactly is your product/service?

How is it different from other products/ service in the market?

Is it different because it is faster (saves time), cheaper (saves money) or better (more efficient)? Be specific

6. What value are you creating?

B. INDUSTRY INSIGHT &ANALYSIS

Now, let us take a wider look at your value proposition. Let us consider the industry of the proposed business and look at factors that can influence the market including competitors.

7. Which industry does this business operate in?

You will need to identify the primary industry you will operate in. Some products or service will cross across more than one industry for example a business making teaching aids for science practical classes from plastic can be classed as being in the educational sector and as well as the manufacturing sector. However, the primary sector in this case is the educational sector since that is the primary benefit of the product. Choosing the industry is critical as it defines many things.

8. How big is the industry?

How much units of products is produced nationwide (volume) and how much money is made nationwide (value)? How fast does the industry grow? This information is usually not readily available. You will need to do a lot of research to get this information. You might not get the information you need from one single source but you can find vital information from different sources such as industry news, industry magazines and financial reports. You can get information from government websites such as the Central Bank, Bureau of Statistics and the National Population Commission.

9. What are the top three things that guarantee success in this industry?

Here you try to find out from the research into the industry, the critical success factors for businesses in that particular industry. You need to know this if you intend to succeed in your own venture. Getting this information might not be as difficult as you can simply ask people who are already running a business in the industry to share their experience.

10. Who are the biggest players in the industry? What are they getting right or wrong?

As a follow up to the previous question, Identifying the biggest players in the industry gives you the opportunity to study the companies who are already succeeding and not only that dominating the market in a business you want to venture into. The benefits of doing this cannot be overemphasized. You learn what they are doing right that you can replicate in your business and you learn what they are not doing too well about and you can take advantage of that to position yourself.

11. What advantage will your own business have over them?

Having considered the strengths and weaknesses of your biggest competitors, how are you going to leverage on their weakness for your advantage? How will you fill the gaps that they have not filled so your own business becomes relevant and valuable to people? You need to think hard on this differentiating value because it lies at the centre of your success in business.

12. What strategy will you use (whether in production/ operations, marketing, sales, recruitment, e.t.c.) that will guarantee your success among the competition?

Sometimes, the advantage your business will have over others in the industry is in your strategy for operating the business, recruitment, production methods, marketing and so on.

C. ANALYSE THE MARKET

13. Who is your customer?

Describe your customer in full giving specific details such as Name, Age, Sex, Work, School, Location (village, town, city, rural, urban), family type (big, small, polygamy),

14. Where will you find my customers?

Now that you have identified your customers, where is the exact location(s) to find them so you can share information about your products and services with them?

15. What other places, things or themes are associated with your customers? What issues bring them together?

Think about and list out common attributes of your typical customers. What other attributes within and outside your product, service or industry is generally common to people like your typical customer you have identified above. I.e. People who do sports will probably shop for sport wears.

16. What is the size and growth potential of your customers size?

Can you estimate the size of your customers within the particular geography that you cover? Is this market a growing and increasing market or it is a declining market with less and less persons needing the product or service. Give percentages and figures. Check industry magazines, websites, to get accurate figures.

17. How will I ensure they see and hear about my product/service?

In this crowded and competitive 21st century markets, getting in front of your customers is one thing and catching their attention is another thing. How do you think you can effectively catch the attention of your customers while they go about their busy lives and daily activities?

18. Why will your potential customers buy from you and not your competitor?

Since you are not the first person to offer them a good solution and there are tens of alternatives in the market, why would they leave their current brands and buy from you or patronize you. Why will they walk past 10 other shops selling the same things as you and buy from only you. How will you build loyalty for your brand?

19. How much are they willing to pay for the product/service?

You have a great product and the entire plan sounds great. However, are your customers willing to pay for that product or service? Likewise, are they able to afford it? If your target customers are not willing to pay or cannot afford the solution, you will have no business. You will need to strike a balance between the value you propose and the pricing to crack this code. Note that this does not suggest that your product or service has to be cheap. For example, a Uber ride is affordable to a bank manager but might be too expensive for someone who hawks and sells gala in the traffic. So you see this too is actually about your customer and understanding their purchasing power and priorities.

20. How exactly will you make profit?

Sometimes some ideas can sound so great and yet, there is no clarity in how the owner will actually make enough money from the business. Think about this and identify specifically the one or many ways by which you can make money providing the product or service.

21. Who is the user of your product? Is the user the same person likely to pay for the product/ service?

Sometimes, the user is not the person who pays. If you were selling school bags for example. The users are school aged children but they will not be the ones most likely to buy your product. Your bag products would be purchase by parents sometimes when the users (children) are not present.

Understanding who pays for your product or service helps you properly position your brand and market yourself so you reach the target audience effectively.

22. Is your product or service targeted to your local neighborhood or your customers can be found throughout the country or continent?

D. FINANCE & FINANCIALS

23. How much capital do I need to raise or invest for the business to take off / start?

Have you figured out how much you need to invest before you can start the business? But just before you think about that, be aware that some businesses literarily do not need any amount to start.

Good will is also a currency that is sometimes more valuable than cash. You could even structure your business model such that it is not cash dependent. i.e. being a middle man for buyer and seller.

How much do you need to get it off the ground? What is the minimum amount? While some businesses do not require any equipment to get it off the ground, some others cannot kick off until they get a couple of equipment and machineries.

24. Where will I get the required capital from?

As you begin to figure out how much you need, you obviously need to begin to figure out how and where you will raise the money. Are you relying on personal savings or intend to get investors starting off from family and friends? Do you want to apply for business grants and pitch for investment from venture capitalists? Will you consider a loan facility?

25. What percentage of the required funds will you generate from all of the sources?

The answer to these question is vital because aside the fact that it is included in a business plan.

26. How much do I need to invest in the business to produce the first unit of my product (1 product)/ or get my first paying customer?

Here you need to talk in units of your products or service. How much will it cost to produce one unit? To get this, you might need to use a formula i.e. Total cost of production divided by Total number of goods produced is equals to the cost of producing one unit.

Remember to factor in all associated cost for the product and not only the obvious one. For example, wages, marketing.

27. How much will I make on each product/ from each service?

Thinking in unit cost helps to see the profitability of the business as you can easily determine if the profit mark-up is ideal compared to the market prices. You should then begin to set prices for all the products and determine how much profit you will make from each. A lot of market research is required to get this right and it is also fine to make informed assumptions.

28. How much product/ service will I sell per month and per year?

If you make assumptions based on the demand for your product and service and considering other market forces, you can begin to estimate how much of this product/ service you will sell per day, week, month and year. This will tie into the market size you have identified previously. With a known ideal customer and market size, how many products will you sell over time? The answer to this question shows if indeed the business is profitable on the long run.

I will like to say one more thing here and it applies to every time you are making assumptions. There is what is called conservative estimates. Conservative estimates is about painting the worst case scenario if everything does not go as planned and sales do not move as expected.

It is valuable to make estimates on both extremes. Worst case scenario and best case scenario. While best case scenarios help us see the maximum profit making potential in a business, making a plan only on Best case scenario can affect business entirely if for a few period, business do not pick up as expected.

29. How much will I need to spend monthly even if I do not make any sales?

This is where you consider your running costs which are not dependent on sales. You might have to pay rent and wages even if you do not make any sales.

Thinking about all these helps you to design your business model to favor maximum profit. If you realize renting a place would not help the business, you can therefore consider shared offices or taking the business completely online.

30. How long will it take to make back the money invested in the business?

You can do some calculations for this. You know how much you invested; you know how much you sell one product. You know how much profit you will make and you know how much it will cost you to run the business. The next thing then is how long it will take you to make back your investment.

E. MANAGEMENT

One of the reasons businesses fail is because of lack of proper management. Indeed, no matter how great an idea is, without the right team and leadership, it might not take off and if it does, it is bound to fail in no distant time.

Investors and funders usually invest in people and not even in the business itself. If they are convinced you have the skills, experience and expertise to run the business you have a higher chance of getting a YES to your request for funding.

Another very important part of this puzzle is integrity. If people realize you can be trusted with money and that you are a wo(man) of integrity, they are more likely to invest in you and your ideas and to buy from you.

31. Which previous experience do you have in leadership and people management?

This is similar to the previous question, but this focuses on your leadership experience. Have you ever led a group, team, association, company in any capacity? Do you have leadership experience in the business environment or work place? Managing people from different backgrounds, cultures and beliefs can be a lot of work. Knowing that you have successfully managed a team of people in the past is a great relief that you can do more in the future.

32. What skill/ experience do I have to run this business successfully?

The particular business you want to venture into probably requires some set of skills and expertise. Maybe it only needs having some basic knowledge or a more advanced knowledge and/or practical hands on experience. Do you have these skills and experience? If you do, then by all means list them out convincingly. If you don't at a first glance, think again, are there transferable skills you can bank on from your past work and life experience?

33. What skill do you need to run the business that I do not have?

While it is lovely to have all the skills required to run this business idea of yours, being able to identify the important skills and that you are aware that you currently lack these skills is a plus. But it doesn't end there and this leads us to the next thought in the next question.

34. How do you intend filling the skill gap?

Now that you have identified some gaps in knowledge, skills and expertise, how do you plan to fill these gaps? Will you go for more learning maybe in a formal classroom or by shadowing someone already in the business? Will you seek paid employment in an organization in the line of your proposed business? Will you partner with other people that have what you lack to run the business? Will you rather employ someone who can fill in this gap so you do not have to worry about it? How best will you fill the identified gaps?

35. Do you require any partnerships to succeed in this business?

While I talked of partnerships above in the context of filling skill and expertise gaps, there are some businesses that that require strategic partnership to succeed. Partnerships can also be a marketing strategy but in this context, partnerships are vital to determine whether the business will even take off or not. If your business does require partnership at this level, have you identified potential partners?

36. Do you require any patents, licensing, and accreditation to start or grow the business?

Similar to the above question but focusing on legal obligations. Do you need to get patents, copyrights, accreditation, licenses and permits to start the business? If yes, what are the requirements to meet these obligations?

F. EXTERNAL FACTORS

Things like skills, leadership experience are internal factors that are dependent on you. However, there are many other factors that are outside your control and power and these factors ultimately determine whether you will succeed in the business venture. You will need to understand how this many numerous external factors can affect your business so that you are empowered to make the right business decisions.

Many factors affect the take off and growth of a business and we have discussed a lot of them already. Many of these factors are internal. That means, you have control over what you do and do not do. However, there are other factors which are external to the business but have a huge impact on your results.

We will now evaluate some of these factors and it is important you consider them and understand how these factors can impact and influence your business.

The known external factors are generally grouped into four areas as follows with an acronym viz. The PEST Analysis.

37. Are there any Political factors/ issues that can affect your business and industry, positively or negatively?
Are there any government regulations, tax policies, legal issues, bureaucracy that can affect your business? Is there stability in the political sector?

How will elections and governance affect your business in the short and long term, positively or negatively?

38. Are there any likely Economic issues/ tends that can affect your business and industry, positively or negatively?
What are the inflation and interest rates? How will they affect you?

What about unemployment, cost of labor, income levels and globalization?

39. Are they any occurrence or trends in the public media and social media space that can affect your business and industry be it positively or negatively?

Population growth, health literacy levels, education, lifestyle choices, press attitude, public opinion and so on are different factors that can influence the success of a business.

40. How will current and future technology affects your business and industry, positively or negatively?

With the internet of things (IoT) take over, the impact of emerging technologies should not be overlooked. On the basic level, you should consider how access to the internet can impact your business and on a deeper level, will your business exist in the next 10 to 20 years.

You should also consider how much research and development is going into your industry and sector.

Are people coming up with innovations by the minute?

How can you position yourself to maximize all the benefit of Technology?

With the purchase of this guide, you get a complimentary access to our entire Business Planning Toolkit

Access Link:
https://drive.google.com/open?id=141rkZEXGXoX1Jwrj7W5Zl6yfBoz15R_e

OR http://bit.ly/BPToolkit2

Contents:
- The 40 Questions Business Planning Workbook
- 4 Unique Business Plan Templates (1 Basic, 2 Intermediate, 1 Advanced templates)
- Cashflow Projection Financial Template on Excel with notes and automated formulas
- Marketing Plan Template

40 Questions Business Planning Workbook

The Business Planning Toolkit which includes 4 Business Plan Templates Excel Cash Flow & Marketing Plan Templates

Notes:

I recommend you read the **Business Planning Guide** first while you either take notes in your personal notepad or you take notes on the **workbook** especially if you are working on a device. You can as well print the workbook and answer the questions on the hard copy. For best results, use the Planning Guide in two ways. The first time you read it, you can read through from start to finish noting down your thoughts. But you need to read a second time, spending at least 24 hours to answer each question. You can take longer for more critical thinking and planning of your business ideas.

When you are done with filling the Workbook, you can then choose any of the **Business Plan Templates**(depending on the purpose of the plan) and fill out the sections. The **Marketing Plan** also comes handy at this time and lastly, you fill the **Cash flow projection** ensuring that it ties to the financial information in your business plan. The first sheet in the Cash flow projection contains a detailed explanation of the items on the cash flow. Simply follow them to enter accurate figures.

Using the Workbook and Templates

Provide answers to these 40 questions in the Business Planning Workbook provided and draw inferences from the various related sections. Spend a few more days brooding over your answers and then proceed to use any of the Business plan templates to write out your business plan from scratch.

If you have answered the questions to a good detail, all you need to do is to copy your responses on the workbook and paste them into the plan in the relevant section.

You then later on, edit and tie it up together.

Other Books by the Author

THE WINNING CV BLUEPRINT

Learn to write CVs employers cannot ignore even if you are a recent graduate with no work experience

In the WINNING CV BLUEPRINT, you will learn:

- How to write a job landing CV from scratch.
- How to think like the employer and write a CV that stands out
- How to communicate your skills and experience so that employers can shortlist you for an interview.
- How to edit your CV for every job you are applying for in a way that presents you as the best candidate.
- How to handle job applications and use it to your advantage if you have limited job experience, are changing career or have employment gap
- And so much more.

The Winning CV Blueprint is a hands-on practical guide to teach students, recent graduates and young professionals how to sell themselves as an ideal candidate for any job.

This book was written from a first-hand experience of applying and interviewing for numerous jobs going on to get 5 well paying jobs within a space of 5 years across two continents and having helped countless number of people review their CVs and applications to get a job or win a competition.

Purchase on Amazone through the ink below
https://www.amazon.com/dp/B07DM5JVVX

www.ingramcontent.com/pod-product-compliance
Lightning Source LLC
Chambersburg PA
CBHW031506210526
45463CB00003B/1096